HAL•LEONARD
INSTRUMENTAL PLAY-ALONG

AUDIO
ACCESS
INCLUDED

PLAYBACK+
Speed • Pitch • Balance • Loop

VIOLA

Movie and TV Music

Audio Arrangements by Peter Deneff

To access audio visit:
www.halleonard.com/mylibrary

Enter Code
3520-9456-4437-7583

ISBN 978-1-5400-2070-3

HAL•LEONARD®

Visit Hal Leonard Online at
www.halleonard.com

Contact Us:
Hal Leonard
7777 West Bluemound Road
Milwaukee, WI 53213
Email: info@halleonard.com

In Europe contact:
Hal Leonard Europe Limited
Distribution Centre, Newmarket Road
Bury St Edmunds, Suffolk, IP33 3YB
Email: info@halleonardeurope.com

In Australia contact:
Hal Leonard Australia Pty. Ltd.
4 Lentara Court
Cheltenham, Victoria, 3192 Australia
Email: info@halleonard.com.au

THE AVENGERS
from THE AVENGERS

VIOLA

Composed by
ALAN SILVESTRI

CAPTAIN AMERICA MARCH

from CAPTAIN AMERICA

VIOLA

By ALAN SILVESTRI

DOCTOR WHO XI

VIOLA

By MURRAY GOLD

DOWNTON ABBEY
(Theme)

VIOLA

Music by JOHN LUNN

GAME OF THRONES
Theme from the HBO Series GAME OF THRONES

VIOLA

By RAMIN DJAWADI

GUARDIANS OF THE GALAXY
from GUARDIANS OF THE GALAXY

VIOLA

Composed by TYLER BATES,
DIETER HARTMANN, TIMOTHY WILLIAMS
and KURT OLDMAN

HAWAII FIVE-O THEME

from the Television Series

VIOLA

By MORT STEVENS

MARRIED LIFE

from UP

VIOLA

By MICHAEL GIACCHINO

Moderately

Sax and clarinet

OUTLANDER THEME
(The Skye Boat Song)

VIOLA

Traditional Music
Arranged by BEAR McCREARY

PROLOGUE AND PROLOGUE PART 2

from BEAUTY AND THE BEAST

Viola

PROLOGUE
Music by ALAN MENKEN

PROLOGUE PART 2
Music by ALAN MENKEN and CHRISTOPHER BENSTEAD

REY'S THEME
from STAR WARS: THE FORCE AWAKENS

VIOLA

Music by JOHN WILLIAMS

THEME FROM THE X-FILES

from the Twentieth Century Fox Television Series THE X-FILES

VIOLA

By MARK SNOW

TEST DRIVE
from the Motion Picture HOW TO TRAIN YOUR DRAGON

VIOLA

By JOHN POWELL